THEN & NOW

MCHENRY

Sandra Landen Machaj

This book is dedicated to the following: the city of McHenry as it celebrates its 175th birthday, Pat Schafer and Marya Dixon for their many hours of sharing memories of McHenry and their help in gathering materials for this book, and the McHenry Area Historical Society and the McHenry County Historical Society for their work in preserving McHenry's history.

Copyright © 2011 by Sandra Landen Machaj
ISBN 978-0-7385-8299-3

Library of Congress Control Number: 2011922180

Published by Arcadia Publishing
Charleston, South Carolina

Printed in the United States of America

For all general information, please contact Arcadia Publishing:
Telephone 843-853-2070
Fax 843-853-0044
E-mail sales@arcadiapublishing.com
For customer service and orders:
Toll-Free 1-888-313-2665

Visit us on the Internet at www.arcadiapublishing.com

ON THE FRONT COVER: The trestle bridge over the Fox River was built in 1881. It was not only the way to cross the Fox River into downtown McHenry, it was also the best place to watch the boat races on the river. Boat races were often part of the summer festivals. The original bridge was replaced in 1977 to accommodate wider automobiles. Because the original bridge is so fondly remembered, plans are being considered to install one section of the old bridge over Boone Creek on the Riverwalk. (Then, courtesy of the McHenry County Historical Society; now, author's collection.)

ON THE BACK COVER: Celebrations and parades are a part of life in McHenry. The summer festival, originally called Marine Days, sponsored a parade representing businesses and organizations in the city and was a favorite of residents. The summer festival's name was changed to Fiesta Days, and the parades continue. This float represents the milk industry, an important part of the history of McHenry. (Courtesy of the McHenry Area Historical Society.)

CONTENTS

ACKNOWLEDGMENTS

Compiling a history of change, especially one spanning over 175 years, is a monumental task, and it cannot be completed alone. I have met many people, both past and present residents of McHenry, who have made it possible to better understand the changes in McHenry over the years by sharing both memories and photographs of the city.

Without Patricia Schafer, this book would not be. Her unending enthusiasm, energy, and assistance in procuring information and her ability to always pull another source out of nowhere is beyond description. With Marya Dixon, we have travelled the streets of McHenry, taking and retaking photographs and interviewing so many.

Special thanks go to the participants of our discussion groups, Ron Conway, Marya Dixon, Don Doherty, Carole Ficken Barb Gilpin, Shirley Klapperich, Larry Phalin, Pat Schafer, and Don Wattles, who shared so many memories of growing up in McHenry. Some of them made me laugh; others taught me to appreciate the closeness of the community and made me wish I had been a part of those times.

Thank you, Kay Bates of the McHenry Area Chamber of Commerce, for suggesting that I put this book together to celebrate McHenry's 175th birthday.

The City of McHenry has been so supportive of this work. Thank you, Bill Hobson, for the photographs of city hall. Mayor Sue Low, thank you for your help in finding a much needed photograph.

I would especially like to recognize Ethel Blake, Ed Buss, Buss Ford employees, Ron Bykowski, Joan Chase, Lil Cairns, Mike Clark, Suzanne Cannon, Dennis Conway, Ron Conway, Marya Dixon, Don Doherty, Nancy Fike, Carole Ficken, Kathleen Giamalva, Bill Hobson, Dorothy Howard, Barb Gilpin, Shirley Klapperich, Marlene Keenan, Mayor Sue Low, Ron Mrachek, Marian Olson, Michele Peterson, Larry Phalin, Ruth Wohnrade, Jean and Vern Schiller, Alyce and John Shay, Dorothy Stoffel, Don Wattles, Don Weingart, Bill and Mary Lou Weber, Marie Wilt, Patrick Wirtz, Ilene Wiedemann, Carol Zank, and anyone I may have inadvertently left out. While not all contributions were used in the book because of space limitations, they are still appreciated.

As usual, the resources of the McHenry County Historical Society and the McHenry Area Historical Society were vital in completing this book. Their work is necessary to keep the history of McHenry alive for future generations.

Unless otherwise noted, modern images are from the author's collection.

INTRODUCTION

This year, 2011, the city of McHenry celebrates its 175th birthday. It has been 175 years since Dr. Christy Wheeler, generally recognized as the first settler, built his home on the banks of the Fox River, starting the growth of a city, known today as McHenry.

What changes have occurred in the past 175 years in McHenry? What would the early settlers think of the McHenry of today? Would they be favorably impressed? Let us take a look at the city from their perspective.

Christy Wheeler was considered the first doctor in McHenry despite having no formal medical training. Can you imagine the look on his face if he were able to see modern medicine today in McHenry? The Centegra Hospital, with its laboratories, radiological facilities, emergency services, and multitudes of specialty doctors who practice the latest modern medicine has to offer, provides a very different service than Wheeler was able to offer.

Wheeler also opened a small store. The number of stores currently in downtown McHenry and the explosive growth of the mega stores on Richmond Road could not have been imagined in 1836 or even in 1900.

Benjamin B. Brown, who is credited with starting the first school in his two-room log cabin at the riverfront, would certainly be overwhelmed by the schools of McHenry today. With a public school elementary district consisting of eight separate school buildings and an enrollment of approximately 5,500 students, a high school district with two campuses educating 2,526 students, and a parochial school, it is a far different educational system then was found in Brown's day.

When George Gage brought the railroad to McHenry in 1854, it ultimately carried many visitors to the city, many of who came for the resorts on the river and to visit the lotus beds. The railroad later served as a commuter train for residents who were employed in the city of Chicago. Today, the railroad trains still come to McHenry, but service is very limited. While Gage might be disappointed that his railroad is not as popular as it once was, he would be pleased that many of the homes of his era, including his own home on Main Street, are still wonderful homes for people of the community.

Page Colby, who built his home and farm along McCullom Lake Road in the mid-1800s, would be surprised at how few farms are left in the area, but he would probably be pleased that his farm still stands and is being preserved by the City of McHenry as the Colby-Petersen Farm and used as a place to allow succeeding generations a glimpse of past farm life.

How would any of these early settlers view the many changes that have occurred since the 1880s? Could they even imagine indoor plumbing, gas furnaces, electric lights, gas and electric stoves, microwave ovens, washing machines, and dryers? Would they believe that horses are rare and only used for pleasure riding, no longer the means of plowing the fields or providing transportation to town and church? They would be surprised that roads are now paved, automobiles are the way to get from one place to another, and that people are more likely to take an airplane than a train to travel across the country.

Even more amazing would be that their country has sent people to the moon. They would be awed at how life has changed, with computers incorporated in every area of life. Many people have not one television in their homes, but one in every room. Children have their own telephones, and there are no family party lines as there were in the early days of telephones.

In this book, we will look at some of the physical changes to the city of McHenry over the past 175 years. We will look at its growth and change and revisit some of the losses that McHenry has experienced.

Today, McHenry has changed from the river town and fledgling frontier county seat of 1836. It has adapted to change throughout the years, just as the entire country has done. It has embraced growth and technology while still working to maintain the warmth and friendliness of the small town on the river that it has always been. As McHenry begins its next era working toward its 200th birthday, more changes will occur, but there is no doubt that McHenry will continue to honor its heritage and remain the city on the Fox River, proud of its past and looking forward to its future. The river was and continues to be an important part of the life of McHenry residents. Just as the many bridges of McHenry connect one section of town to another, we the people of McHenry are the bridge connecting the past with the present.

Happy birthday McHenry!

DOWN BY
THE RIVERSIDE

BOAT RACE, SEPT. 19TH 1909
AT McHENRY, ILL

The waterfront, site of the first cabin here, is the heart of McHenry. Visitors and residents enjoyed activities on the water, including rides on excursion boats, watching boat races, and staying at the resorts found along its shores. Restaurants, taverns, hotels, and dance halls, along with grocery stores and ice-cream parlors, flourished here. (Courtesy of the McHenry County Historical Society.)

This brick building, located on the northeast corner of Riverside Drive and Pearl Street, was constructed in 1903. The structure was originally built to house an electrical power-generating and distribution station for McHenry. The third floor of the building was used as a dance hall before becoming a roller rink. Other businesses here included a Model T assembly garage, a tent maker, a dress factory, and a wine boutique. Tents were manufactured for World War II in this building. (Then, courtesy of Don Howard.)

Built in 1889, the Barbian home (far left) is one of the oldest homes still in existence along North Riverside Drive. Located north of downtown McHenry, the road follows the river towards Johnsburg. The Barbian brothers began a cigar-manufacturing business in McHenry in 1876. The cigars produced here were sold under the label Our Monogram. They were hand rolled in the one-story rear portion of the home. (Then, courtesy of Patricia Blake Schafer.)

This building was originally located in the area that now is Veteran's Park and was built to serve as the county courthouse. When the county seat was moved to Woodstock, the building was sold and moved to the corner of Pearl Street and Riverside Drive. As J.C. Bickler's McHenry House, it was a popular hotel and buffet. It later became known as Automobile Headquarters. Ownership has changed over the years and is now in business as the Town Club. (Then, courtesy of Michael Clark.)

Riverside Motor Sales was owned by Albert Blake. The agency sold Packard automobiles and was directly across from the Chrysler dealership on the other side of Pearl Street. With the movement of the automobile dealerships away from Pearl, the building was rented. For over 40 years, the Hostess Company rented the building, providing Hostess products, such as bread and Twinkies, to residents of McHenry. (Then, courtesy of Patricia Blake Schafer.)

The Old Bridge Tavern, originally Buch's Hotel, is located on the southeast corner of Pearl Street and Riverside Drive. It is a historic building believed to be one of the oldest (if not the oldest) frame structures in McHenry. Prior to World War II, a decorative metallic widow's walk was located on the roof. The metal was removed during the conflict to be used for the war effort. (Then, courtesy of the McHenry Area Historical Society.)

Buch's Place, McHenry, Ill.

6110.

Today, it seems that on every corner there is a drugstore, while in the 1940s and 1950s it seemed that every corner held a gasoline station. The corners of Elm Street and Riverside Drive were home to two such stations. Holly's Texaco Station was located on the southeast corner, while the Standard Oil Station was found on the northwest corner. Gasoline was pumped, oil was checked, and windows were washed with every purchase. A jewelry and coin shop has replaced the Standard Station. (Then, courtesy of McHenry Area Historical Society.)

This elegant hotel was built on the corner of Riverside Drive and Elm Street in the 1860s using bricks made from clay harvested from the clay hole located at the end of Riverside Drive. Ownership, accompanied by name changes, occurred over the years. A ballroom on the third floor of this hotel held dances, wedding receptions, anniversaries, and other gala occasions. It even presented professional entertainment. (Then, courtesy of Patrick Wirtz.)

Riverside Drive was not only a place for visitors, it was also the shopping center for those who lived in this section of town. A drugstore was located here for many years, first as the popular Nye Drugs and later, with a change of ownership, McHenry Drugs. Today, this location is the home of Riverside Shop-n-Go. (Then, courtesy of Patricia Blake Schafer.)

In 1934, Holly's Filling Station and Ice House opened in this building, believed to have been constructed around 1890. McHenry residents continued to purchase their gasoline from Warren Holly until 1974. In 1976, Harriet Whitman, along with Don and Kathy Schramm, opened the Windhill Pancake Parlor in this former gas station. The restaurant has remained a favorite spot for breakfast for residents of McHenry and surrounding towns. (Then, courtesy of the McHenry County Historical Society.)

Owned by Ma and Pa Schimmel and located on River Road next to the Fox River, Snug Harbor opened for business in 1933. The Springmans purchased the restaurant in 1946 and operated it until 1956. Subsequent owners added a glass porch facing the river. After a period of being closed and then remodeled, it reopened in 2009. In 2011, the name was changed to the Snuggery. (Then, courtesy of Marian Olson.)

Travel throughout McHenry changed with the building of the new bridge over the Fox River at Elm Street in 1927. Prior to the construction of the Elm Street Bridge, the only way to cross the river to visit the east side of town was to do it via boat. With the new bridge, the traffic pattern changed, and Elm Street (Route 120) became the major east–west street through town. (Then, courtesy of Ilene Wiedemann.)

DOWN BY THE RIVERSIDE

A favorite leisure sports activity that brought friends out was bowling. Bowling alleys could be found in various places throughout town. The alleys in the 1900s were not the mega complexes found today. Instead, they consisted of one to four lanes and were often associated with a restaurant and bar. Schaefer's Tavern, owned by brothers Herman and Ambrose Schaefer, added their four lanes in 1937. They sold the business in 1950. Today, the bowling alley is still used by residents and has been increased to 12 lanes. (Then, courtesy of Ruth Wohnrade.)

This was an empty lot on the southwest corner of River Road and Pearl Street, along the east side of the Fox River, until a small A-frame building was constructed here. Today, that building houses Vickie's Place, a popular waterfront restaurant. On warm summer days, customers arrive by automobile or by boat for a pleasant meal on the patio. (Then, courtesy Shirley Klapperich.)

The Hunter Boat Company, the largest of the local boat companies in McHenry, loomed on the eastern shores of the Fox River. Hunter was known for many types of boats, including solid mahogany crafts. It built and operated the excursion boats that traveled the Fox River up to the Chain of Lakes, providing employment to many local residents. Hunter sponsored the popular boat races along the river, and boat owners were always proud to earn one of the Hunter-supplied trophies. (Then, courtesy of the McHenry County Historical Society.)

The Riverside Bakery has been in McHenry for many years. It is presently owned and operated by the Rice family, who has been at this location for over 40 years. Many McHenry residents have fond memories of beautiful birthday cakes with rich frosting. Breads, donuts, and pastries always taste better when fresh from the bakery. The awnings have been replaced by shake shingles, but the quality inside remains the same. (Then, courtesy of Patricia Blake Schafer.)

CHAPTER 2

STROLLING THE CENTER

Green Street, located in the section of town known as Centerville, grew into its own retail area, including grocery stores, banks, restaurants, a movie theater, schools, and city hall. Travel between West McHenry and Riverside Drive required a drive down Green Street. (Courtesy of the McHenry Area Historical Society.)

Pictured is the building on the southeast corner of Green and Elm Streets. It was originally a grocery store. At the time of this photograph, it had become part of the certified chain of grocery stores. The parade passing by was well attended, as such events in McHenry always were and continue to be today. The building is currently in use as a bar and pizza restaurant. (Both courtesy of Patricia Blake Schafer.)

This young man is enjoying the snow tunnel in front of the Hoy Bank sometime around 1929. The Hoy Bank came into existence in 1913, when Clarence and Fremont Hoy purchased the Bank of McHenry. The building is now the home of the McHenry Area Chamber of Commerce. It was formed in 1952 when the McHenry Businessmen's Association voted to become the McHenry Area Chamber of Commerce. Photographed below at the building are, from left to right, assistant membership director Bonnie Curry, president Kay Rial Bates, and events director Jane Manny. (Then, courtesy of McHenry County Historical Society.)

Bishop's Mill on Green Street is believed to have been built on the site of the original Owen's Mill. Many residents recognize this as the site of Gladstone's Department Store. In the basement of Gladstone's, the Switzer Boat Factory built many of the Switzer Crafts found travelling up and down the river. Today, Green Street Café is found here. (Then, courtesy of the McHenry County Historic Society.)

This building, located at 1209 North Green Street, became the American Legion Hall on November 13, 1949. After serving as the Legion Hall, the building was sold to the McHenry Savings Bank in 1965. After some remodeling to make the building suitable for a bank, a grand opening was held on June 3, 1967. The bank continues to serve the community at this location. The front of the building has changed; it has a newly designed front, and drive-through banking has been added. (Then, courtesy of McHenry Area Historical Society.)

In the 1920s, movies were a favorite pastime, and McHenry residents enjoyed their favorites at the Empire Theatre on Green Street. The venue was built and operated by J.W. and Mattie Smith in 1929. The name changed to the Colony Theatre in 1939 and remained the Colony until 1952, when it was destroyed by fire. The McHenry Theatre was rebuilt in 1955 with funding furnished by A.P. Freund, Morris Gladstone, and Dr. Lee Gladstone. It continues to provide popular movies to the community. (Then, courtesy of Michael Clark.)

Because of its proximity to water, bridges have played an important role in allowing residents to roam the city. The new bridge constructed on Green Street over Boone Creek was dedicated on May 20, 1949. Because of the presence of the millpond, Elm Street as it is known today was not a through street. Visitors traveling from West McHenry to Riverside Drive went down Main Street to Green Street, crossing the bridge over Boone Creek and continuing on to Pearl Street. (Both courtesy of Patricia Blake Schafer.)

The look along Boone Creek has changed in the past 10 years, as the Riverwalk has been developed along its shores. With walkways and gazebos, spending a few hours strolling along the shores is a great way to spend an afternoon. The initial phase was completed in 2006. The walk will be extended along the shore of the Fox River from Green Street to Riverside Drive. (Both courtesy of the City of McHenry.)

The look and use of the space on Green Street along Boone Creek has changed dramatically since this photograph was taken in the 1950s. Originally the site of Dr. Gladstone's office, the hospital opened on the lower level. In 1966, an adjoining three-story building was constructed in response to growing needs. In 1984, the hospital moved to a larger facility located on Bull Valley Road. Today, a mixed-use building containing retail businesses on the ground level and condominiums on the upper levels occupies this site. (Then, courtesy Marie Wilt.)

The first city hall of McHenry is believed to have been in the old cheese factory, which was located on Green Street. By the early 1900s, it became necessary to consider a new city hall. The new structure was built in 1920, faced with white terra-cotta tiles manufactured by the American Terra Cotta Company, located on Route 31. (Then, courtesy of the City of McHenry.)

City Hall, McHenry, Ill.

STROLLING THE CENTER

The McHenry city government moved to this larger facility on south Green Street in 1991. Today, it continues to be home to many city services. Gathered for this photograph are, from left to right, Rich Wimmer (alderman), Jeff Schaefer (alderman), Chris Black (city administrator), Sue Low (mayor), Ryan Schwalenberg (director of construction and neighborhood service), Bill Hobson (assistant city administrator), and John Jones (police chief). (Then, courtesy of the City of McHenry.)

Armistice Day
Nov. 11 1925

People gathered in front of the William Tesch house to celebrate Armistice Day in 1925. The Tesch house was purchased in 1952 to be the library. Volunteers remodeled the building at no charge. By 1965, an addition was completed to house the growing collection. When the library moved to a larger location on Front Street, the building became the home of School District No. 15. (Then, courtesy of Dennis Conway.)

STROLLING THE CENTER

When the McHenry Country Club opened in 1922 as a private club, it only consisted of a nine-hole golf course. It did not take long to realize the need for a full 18 holes, and in 1926 the additional nine holes were added. The first clubhouse was completed in one day by three men. The current clubhouse was built in 1953 but continues to be remodeled as necessary. Many local brides and grooms remember holding their wedding receptions here. (Then, courtesy of Patricia Schafer.)

McHENRY COUNTRY CLUB, McHENRY

In the early 1900s, farms were plentiful around McHenry, and cows were the most important livestock on a farm. In the photograph below, the cows from the Owens farm are enjoying grazing in the area. Today, it would not be the perfect pasture, as it is John Street and heavily traveled by automobiles. This section is located between fairways for holes one and two of the McHenry Country Club. (Then, courtesy of the McHenry Area Historical Society.)

In 1875, the *Plaindealer*, the newspaper that was to be the voice and reflection of the city of McHenry for over 100 years, began publication. Jay Van Slyke was the founder and owner until 1884. The paper underwent several changes of ownership, and the office of the newspaper changed locations. Adele Froelich was the well-remembered editor. (Then, courtesy of the McHenry County Historical Society.)

George Gribbler founded the McHenry Brewery in 1868. It continued in business up to the 1930s. The beer was produced under several labels. A restaurant opened at this location but remained in business only for a short time. Currently it is empty and up for sale. (Then, courtesy of Michael Clark.)

In the 1840s, visiting priests came to the area to give Mass to local residents. In 1853, a permanent St. Patrick's Church was built (pictured on the far right below). By 1923, the parish had grown due to the increased population of the area, and a new church was needed. The church, completed in 1923, is still in use today. The original church was demolished, and that site is now the parking area for the parish. (Then, courtesy of McHenry Area Historical Society.)

In 1912, this small white church was built on Court Street as the Universalist Church. It was disbanded in 1938, and the church building was donated to the McHenry Masonic Lodge. Today, this building is the home of the Masonic Lodge and has a much different look. The Masonic Lodge was formed and received its charter in 1854. George Gage had the honor of being the first member to sign the membership book on March 27, 1854. (Then, courtesy of McHenry County Historical Society.)

CHAPTER

GROWING TO
THE WEST

The arrival of the Chicago and Northwestern Railroad to Gagetown, or West McHenry as it was later known, spurred the growth of Main Street and Waukegan Road. Grocery stores, hotels, restaurants, hardware stores, a milk factory, and a stockyard grew up quickly in the area to meet the needs of visitors and residents. Homes were built along Main Street and Waukegan Road. (Courtesy of the McHenry Area Historical Society.)

The Stoffel building is located on the northeast corner of Main Street and Route 31. Originally built by George Gage, it has served as Erickson's General Department Store, the home of the first telephone exchange in McHenry, and the spot of Thies' Wholesale Store. On the lower level, a restaurant known as the Nook opened in 1946. The building was remodeled into 11 apartments by Howard Wattles and remains a west-side apartment building. (Then, courtesy of Suzanne Cannon.)

Located on the southeast corner of Main Street and Route 31, this site has been the home of varied businesses. Originally the site of Ben Laure's blacksmith shop, it later became Math Laure's grocery store. Art Smith followed with a grocery store of his own. In the 1950s, the Main Paint Store was located here. Today, a trading-card store is located here. (Then, courtesy McHenry Area Historical Society.)

Teresa Steffan leans out of the upper-floor window overlooking her store, Steffan's. Originally, the store was a record shop and carried some jewelry. Today, Steffan's Jewelry is located on Front Street. McAndrews barbershop, another longtime McHenry business, shared the first building. Today, this space on Main Street is occupied by Plum Garden, the popular restaurant opened by Connie Moy in 1965. It continues the tradition of excellent food, a favorite of McHenry residents under the direction of her son Perry. (Then, courtesy of Suzanne Cannon.)

THE PARK HOTEL
W. McHENRY ILL

The hotel was demolished in September 1947 and replaced with a new garage and automobile showroom by R.I. Overton. Overton conducted his sales of Cadillac automobiles here. The building was then sold to Bruce Eisner. In 1989, it was sold again, and the tenants were the Ashley Corporation and a gymnastics studio. Today, it is occupied by Cash for Gold. (Then, courtesy of the McHenry County Historical Society.)

The Justen Furniture store was opened in 1926 by N.J. Justen. It was taken over by Peter Justen. Later, Peter sold the business to an employee. It was not unusual for the local undertaker to also own the furniture store, especially before 1900, when the undertaker manufactured the caskets and used the extra wood to build furniture. The building was also home to Nielsen's five-and-dime store. After the building burned, the area became a parking lot. (Then, courtesy of Robert Mrachek, Colonial Funeral Home.)

GROWING TO THE WEST

Peter Schaefer grew up north of Johnsburg, but he returned to Chicago, where he was born, in order to work for his brother Ben in his grocery store. In 1918, he opened his own grocery in Chicago, which he sold in 1922 to return to the area. He opened Schaefer's Market on the west end of Main Street. The boardinghouse behind the store was run by Jack Gray. The stockyards were located behind the store on the next block. (Then, courtesy of Dennis Conway.)

The Northwestern Hotel, built in 1901, was located across from the McHenry Train Depot and was often the first stop for arriving travelers before they headed down to the river to enjoy the many water activities available. Among the amenities found at the hotel were a bar and an ice-cream parlor, which also sold cigars. Today, the hotel is rented out as individual apartments. (Then, courtesy of the Ron Conway family.)

GROWING TO THE WEST

In 1854, the Chicago and Northwestern Railroad came to McHenry thanks to state senator George Gage. The train station was located in West McHenry, much of which was owned by Gage. The train brought visitors, many from Chicago, seeking to escape the heat and foul air of the city and to enjoy the country air and activities along the Fox River. Today, Metra trains ride the rails, although service to McHenry is extremely limited. (Then, courtesy of Michael Clark.)

This beautiful building, with its stone foundation and original wood beams, has been standing on Crystal Lake Road since 1870. The Hanly family is listed as one of the early 1836 settlers. Hanly owned and operated the McHenry Flour Mill and Champion Brick Yard from this building. The yellow bricks used to build Landmark School were manufactured here. The structure has had several owners over time. It became a feed mill around 1950 and later was the home of Taylor Made golf clubs. (Then, courtesy of Michael Clark.)

The south side of Main Street had a far different look than it does today. The streets were unpaved, and a small gutter ran along the side. Note the board from the street to the walkway in front of the J. W. Freund store. Today, there are paved streets with cement sidewalks. The stores have changed and cars now line the streets while customers shop or enjoy a meal. (Then, courtesy of McHenry County Historical Society.)

Today, fresh fruits and vegetables are imported from all over the world and available year-round. In the 1800s, vegetables were preserved to make them last through the long, cold Illinois winters. Canning and pickling were very popular ways to preserve food. Vegetables such as cucumbers, cabbage, cauliflower, onions, and tomatoes were purchased from local farmers by the canning factories and placed in brine or vinegar to preserve them. This pickle factory was established in 1874. (Then, courtesy of the McHenry County Historical Society.)

Built in 1872, this Victorian farmhouse with Italianate elements was the home of Harrison and Alsena Smith. Alsena was the daughter of George Gage, the first senator from McHenry. Harrison Smith was a partner in Smith and Snyder Lumber in West McHenry. Today, this picturesque home on West Main Street has been well maintained and is as attractive as it was in the 1800s. (Then, courtesy of McHenry Area Historical Society.)

Founded in 1840, the Methodist Church was one of the early churches in McHenry, first meeting as a prayer group in the home of Ira and Mary Colby, then in a schoolhouse, and later in the Baptist Church. George Gage donated land on West Main Street, where a permanent church was constructed in 1859. The parsonage was added in 1878. Additions in 1938, 1953, and 1979 were made as the congregation grew. (Then, Courtesy of Michael Clark.)

This Gothic Revival–style home, located on Main Street, was the home of George Gage. The home is believed to have been built around 1858. Over the years, additions were added, but the house still retains its early look with its gingerbread trim. The balcony was added in the late 1930s. (Then, courtesy of Bill and Mary Lou Weber.)

This pre–Civil War home, built around 1860, was placed on the National Register of Historic places in 1982 at the request of owners Robert and Marya Dixon because of its architectural significance. Unique features include a front facade on both Waukegan Road and Main Street and original six-by-six windows. The house became the home of Count Oskar Bopp von Oberstadt in the early 1900s and has since been known as the Count's house. It is the only McHenry building on the National Historic Register. (Then, courtesy of Marya Dixon.)

OLD COLONIAL HOME McHENRY ILL.

M163 7

Today, this northeast corner of Waukegan Road and Third Street is an attractive park known as Rotary Park. It has not always been so; prior to 1900, a tall water reservoir standpipe was built here. The pipe can be seen in the background of many old photographs of McHenry, making it easier to pinpoint the photograph's location. The standpipe was dismantled in 1971. (Then, courtesy of the McHenry Area Historical Society.)

Travel south from Main Street was not the straight route that is available today. Front Street ended at John Street, making it necessary to travel east to Green Street and then south to Miller Road before returning to what was then known as Elgin Road (now Route 31). In 1933, workers began the difficult job of extending the road from John Street south to Miller Road (Bull Valley Road), where it connected with Elgin Road. (Then, courtesy of the McHenry Area Historical Society.)

GROWING TO THE WEST

This pristine little church on John Street was dedicated on September 18, 1891, as the home of the Zion Lutheran congregation. The church continued to serve the congregation until 1955, when a larger church was required. The little church was sold to a realtor and Zion Lutheran built a larger facility on Elm Street. The early church was then sold to Alliance Bible Church and subsequently used as a private residence. (Then, courtesy of Dennis Conway.)

Although there were several dance pavilions in McHenry, the most remembered one was the Fox Pavilion, which was located on the east side of the Fox River. After the Fox Pavilion burned around 1930, this new dance pavilion was constructed on Route 31 in West McHenry. While this pavilion was to replace the Fox Pavilion, it was never as popular as the original. In 1947, the building was converted to the McHenry Roller Rink, with a skating surface of 10,000 feet. (Then, courtesy of Shirley Klapperich/Ron Conway families.)

The library continued to grow as residents became more involved in reading and attending children's programs and other literary events offered there. The library, having outgrown the Tesch house on Main and Green Streets, moved to the former Althoff building on Front Street. The addition of computers, research materials, and genealogy materials required more space. In 2010, the building underwent a major renovation in order to accommodate the growing and changing needs of residents. (Then, courtesy of James Althoff.)

In September 1968, McHenry opened its second high school campus, this one on Crystal Lake Road, and Sen. Everett Dirksen was the dedication speaker. Originally, west campus was the home of freshmen and sophomores, while east campus housed juniors and seniors. In 1980, each campus became a four-year facility. Extracurricular activities and sports are provided as district activities, with students from both campuses eligible to participate. In essence, it is one school on two separate campuses. (Then, courtesy of Dr. Carl Valiantos.)

GROWING TO THE WEST

4

CUTTING THROUGH TOWN

In early McHenry, Elm Street was not the through street that it is today. The millpond covered a portion of the area, while the eastern edge of Elm ended at the river. With the draining of the millpond and the construction of the bridge over the Fox River, Elm Street became a major highway for east and west traffic. (Courtesy of Shirley Klapperich.)

Retired farmer Michael Justen built this Queen Anne Revival home in the early 1900s on Elm Street. It was the first house with indoor plumbing to be built in McHenry. In spite of the fact that this house has served as a private residence, a boardinghouse, and a health-food store over the years, it is as attractive now as it was when built. It is currently is the home of a law practice. (Then, courtesy of Shirley Klapperich.)

CUTTING THROUGH TOWN

Built in 1856, this home was a millinery shop owned for 50 years by Mary Fitzsimmons Searles. Following this, the house was a private residence until 1933, when a distributorship for Atlas Prager Beer and a restaurant, the Sip Snack Inn, opened here. Steiny's House of Prager opened in 1961 and remained a popular tavern until it closed in 1985. The building currently contains a law office. (Then, courtesy of Shirley Klapperich/Ron Conway families.)

Most residents of McHenry were very familiar with this classic house located on Elm Street, as it was the home and office of Dr. Charles H. Fegers from 1884 to 1910. He was followed by Dr. Nickolaus Nye, who also practiced medicine and lived in this home. Dr. Nye's second wife was the daughter of Dr. Fegers. Their son, Dr. William Nye, followed his father to become the third physician to practice medicine from this location. (Then, courtesy Ron Conway family.)

Augustino S. Unti operated a tavern on the northeast corner of Green and Elm Streets. This tavern also served as the town's bus station. Augustino's brother Charlie manufactured ice cream, which was also served here. Many bus travelers enjoyed a cool drink or some freshly made ice cream after the long bus ride from the city. The building was torn down, and today the area has been dedicated as a park. (Then, courtesy of Shirley Klapperich.)

Today, the First Midwest Bank, located on Elm Street, occupies much of the block between Richmond Road and Green Street with its large operations building. Originally, a small one-story bank covered a portion of this area, which was the home of the McHenry State Bank. The bank replaced some private houses, including the one containing the offices of Earl Walsh and Dr. Froelich. (Then, courtesy of Patricia Blake Schafer.)

The two busiest highways through downtown McHenry are Route 120 (Elm Street) and Route 31. Driving north on Route 31, it zigzags from Front Street to Elm Street, heading east for a short stretch, before turning north onto Richmond Road. Turning left onto Richmond from Elm is often difficult because of the high volume of traffic. The Illinois Department of Transportation is studying the possibility of widening Richmond as a solution to the traffic jams. (Then, courtesy of McHenry Area Historical Society.)

This Sinclair gasoline station, managed by the Wort's family, was located on the northwest corner of Elm Street and Richmond Road. Today, that corner has a far different look and a far different use. The gasoline station was demolished to make way for the parking lot of the McHenry Fire Department. The main fire station is located directly behind it. (Then, courtesy of Kathie Covalt.)

CUTTING THROUGH TOWN

Everyone has a need to visit Ace Hardware at some time to keep their home in working order. This Ace Hardware, located at 3729 North Elm Street from 1960 to 1989, was the second location for the store. Bjorkman's Ace Hardware then relocated to Crystal Lake Road. Centegra Therapy Services has made this building its home for the past 18 years. (Then, courtesy of Ron Bykowski.)

The first Jewel Food Store arrived in McHenry in 1959 and was located at 3714 Elm Street. Next door was the Millstream Walgreens, a Walgreen Agency drugstore. The Walgreen space was later taken over by Osco Drugs when Jewel purchased Osco. Today, this space is in use by Home of the Sparrow, a resale shop, and Sherwin Williams paint store. (Then, courtesy of Ron Bykowski.)

CUTTING THROUGH TOWN

MB Upholstery shop was opened here by Mitchell Bykowski. His first job was to reupholster the kneelers for St. Mary's Church. In the mid-1950s, an addition was added that became the home of Alyce Joyce Music Studio. It was later used as an attorney's office before becoming the home of Tones Music. Today, it is a part of the Century 21 complex. (Then, courtesy of Ron Bykowski.)

This National Food Store was one of the chain grocery stores that replaced the individually owned grocery stores so prevalent in McHenry. This store was located on Elm Street in the area that previously was part of the millpond. Sullivan's Grocery Store, a favorite of many local residents, followed the National in this space in 1982. Sullivan's closed in 2010 to the dismay of many regular customers. (Then, courtesy of Ron Bykowski.)

CUTTING THROUGH TOWN

Outwardly, other than the addition on the left side, this brick Colonial-style building has shown little change since being constructed in 1939 as the Peter Justen Funeral Home, yet the use of the building has changed dramatically. As seen in the earlier photograph, a 1959 Pontiac hearse is parked in front. Before the rescue squad was established, hearses were used to assist injured people requiring medical care. Currently, the building is the home of Kathryn's Bridal and Dress Shop. (Then, courtesy of Robert G. Mrachek, Colonial Funeral Home.)

Barbecue has been popular among McHenry residents for many generations. Beginning in 1928, John Anderson's Broadway Barbecue was a favorite of many McHenry citizens. The barbeque always was better when it was coupled with a glass of McHenry Beer. While in the area, one could stop for gasoline, which usually cost a total of $1 or $2 since gas costs were often less than 25¢ per gallon. Today, this is the home of the First National Bank of McHenry. (Then, courtesy of the McHenry Area Historical Society.)

CUTTING THROUGH TOWN

Customers looking to purchase a new automobile, especially a Ford, would have started and ended their search at Buss Motors, either on Main Street or Waukegan Road. By the 1960s, the showroom the was located on Elm Street. Today, the agency is located on Route 31, and the former space on Route 120 is now occupied by Walgreens. (Then, courtesy of Buss Ford.)

This building on Borden Drive was the Borden Milk Factory in the early 1900s. From this location, milk would be collected from the local farms and shipped to Chicago by rail. From the millpond, located in front of the building, ice would be cut in winter and used to refrigerate the milk while it was being transported. After the Borden Company moved from McHenry, the Tonyan Construction Company made this building its headquarters. (Then, courtesy of Patricia Schafer.)

CUTTING THROUGH TOWN

Throughout the early to mid-1900s, dancing was a favorite way to socialize. McHenry had several dance pavilions. This one, known as the Bridge, was located on the northeast corner of Elm Street and River Road. Many of the local musicians took part in the live music. Prizefighting was staged, attracting known boxers. Dinners were served for 25¢. In 1950s, the building, like many of the old structures in the area, succumbed to fire. (Then, courtesy of McHenry Area Historical Society.)

Anyone passing the corner of Chapel Hill Road and State Route 120 is sure to notice the uniquely shaped building located on the northwest corner. In the late 1940s, this was the site of the Pine Tree Tower, a favorite place for local teenagers to gather, especially after athletic games, and enjoy hamburgers or ice cream. Today, under the name of the Riverside Chocolate Factory, it is still known for excellent chocolates and ice cream. (Then, courtesy of McHenry County Historical Society.)

CHANGING WITH CHANGE

With neighboring communities on all sides, McHenry is not able to expand by adding additional land to the community but must grow by redeveloping the property that is already part of the city. Shopping centers to the north of town have replaced much of the farmland. The Riverwalk and new buildings are changing the look of the city center. (Courtesy of Vernon and Jean Schiller.)

85

With the construction of Landmark School, the old school building located on Richmond Road next to St. Mary's Catholic Church was sold to the parish to be used as a parochial school. The children of St. Mary's parish attended eight grades here. The building was destroyed in 1936 but replaced. It is now Montini Middle School. The younger grades are being taught at Montini Elementary School, which was formerly St. Patrick's School. (Then, courtesy of Ron Bykowski.)

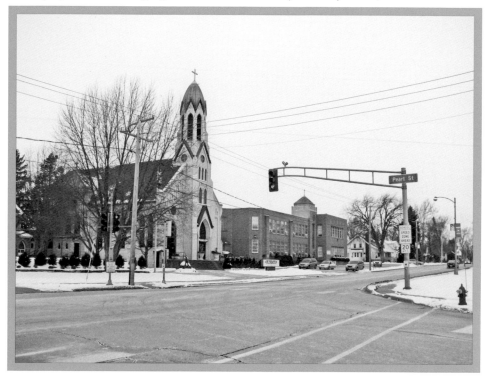

If one visited the corner of Richmond and McCullom Lake Roads 30 years ago, the only things visible were the farmhouse, barn, and fields of Jacob Freund. Today, progress has changed the look of that corner. It is a busy area, with a gasoline station on the corner and a Walmart. (Then, courtesy of Ethel Blake and family.)

Growth along Richmond Road has turned the area that was once a group of neighboring farms into a large shopping area. With strip malls on either side of Richmond Road, many residents head to the multiple malls where the big box stores have made their homes. The farm of William Blake and his son Edward, located on the west side of Richmond Road, was one of the farms located here. Today, the farm has been replaced by Home Depot and Staples. (Then, courtesy of Ethel Blake and family.)

The Blake family farms were found all along what today is Route 31. The Joseph Blake farm was located on the east side of Richmond Road. Today, it no longer exists and has been replaced by a strip mall shopping center. Where the farm once stood there is now a mall that contains such stores as Best Buy and Ultra. (Then, courtesy of Michele Peterson.)

Ben Blake owned another of the family farms located on north Richmond Road that has succumbed to the growth and development of the city. Today, none of the barns, fields, or even the family farmhouse has survived. They have been replaced by another row of retail shops extending from the area of the Burger King to Kohl's Department Store. (Then, courtesy of Jim and Marlene Keenan.)

When Page Colby purchased this land around McCullom Lake in the 1800s and built this farmhouse, it became a working farm for over five generations of the Colby-Petersen family. The farm is now owned by the City of McHenry. On the last Sunday of June, the landmark commission sponsors a Day at Petersen Farm, a festive occasion celebrating life on the farm at different times in history. It is well attended by the community. (Then, courtesy of the McHenry Area Historical Society; now, Patrick Wirtz.)

In the early 1900s, the Shamrock Farm on Draper Road was known for Morgan horse breeding. Over time, its focus changed to dairy farming, hog raising, and then it became a beef cattle feed lot. Under manager Vernon Schiller, 3,200 head of cattle were fed on the lot each year. The farm also grew hay and corn. In 2001, much of the farm was sold, and a housing development replaced the corn and hay fields. (Both courtesy of Vernon and Jean Schiller.)

CHANGING WITH CHANGE

The ___ day of ___ shipping at McHenry Stock Yards ___ and 1912. Compliments of ___ Theo. ___ & ___ Edelweiss B___

Many residents are unaware that McHenry once had stockyards located right in West McHenry. The yard was located on the block behind Pete Schaefer's first store, which would have been Waukegan Street. The yards, which were located near the train tracks, were used to unload cattle from the train and secure them until they could be picked up by the farmers who had ordered them. The stockyards closed around 1930. (Then, courtesy of the McHenry County Historical Society.)

It was a hot summer day, June 9, 1973, when an explosion occurred that rocked homes throughout McHenry and sent up a huge black plume of smoke that could be seen throughout the area. Inside their homes, residents recovered pieces of broken china that had fallen from shelves and spent time clearing the house of broken glass from the blown-out windows. The explosion occurred at World Wide Fireworks, located on McCullom Lake Road. Today, this area is a townhouse subdivision. (Then, courtesy of Dorothy Stoffel.)

This attractive brick building was constructed in 1929 on a floating foundation by Julius Keig. The home was sold to Wallace and Helen Dobyns in 1938. An antiques store operated here until 1989, when the building was sold to Charles Miller. Miller opened Dobyns' House Restaurant and Excursion Boats, known for its daily cruises with meals. Later, it was reopened as Joey T's Restaurant. The building was demolished in 2010 after a fire. (Then, courtesy of the Landmark Commission, City of McHenry.)

DOBYN'S RESIDENCE McHENRY ILL.

WORWICK'S PHOTO

www.arcadiapublishing.com

Discover books about the town where you grew up, the cities where your friends and families live, the town where your parents met, or even that retirement spot you've been dreaming about. Our Web site provides history lovers with exclusive deals, advanced notification about new titles, e-mail alerts of author events, and much more.

MADE IN THE USA

Arcadia Publishing, the leading local history publisher in the United States, is committed to making history accessible and meaningful through publishing books that celebrate and preserve the heritage of America's people and places. Consistent with our mission to preserve history on a local level, this book was printed in South Carolina on American-made paper and manufactured entirely in the United States.

This book carries the accredited Forest Stewardship Council (FSC) label and is printed on 100 percent FSC-certified paper. Products carrying the FSC label are independently certified to assure consumers that they come from forests that are managed to meet the social, economic, and ecological needs of present and future generations.

FSC
Mixed Sources
Product group from well-managed forests and other controlled sources

Cert no. SW-COC-001530
www.fsc.org
© 1996 Forest Stewardship Council

Find Your Place in History.